MW01133363

better together*

*This book is best read together, grownup and kid.

 **akidsco.com**

a
kids
book
about

a kids book about

grief

by Brennan C. Wood
in partnership with Dougy Center

**a
kids
book
about**

A Kids Book About books are available online: *akidsco.com*

To share your stories, ask questions, or inquire about bulk
purchases (schools, libraries, and nonprofits), please use
the following email address: *hello@akidsco.com*

ISBN: 978-1-953955-56-2

Designed by Nakita Simpson
Edited by Emma Wolf

For Jordyn and all the kids like us
who've experienced the life-changing
circumstances of death far too young.

In memory of Doris and Frank Wood—
I live in your legacy of love.

Intro

Grief can be hard to talk about no matter how old you are. It can feel especially difficult to talk about with kids. To protect our kids from feeling loss and grief, we might minimize it, try to take away their pain, shy away from the truth, or avoid talking about it altogether. But we know kids want to have the space and permission to grieve. They want to share their feelings and experiences in their own time, in their own way (which isn't always with words!). They want to know the truth and have their questions answered honestly, even if the honest answer is, "I don't know."

It is a privilege to walk alongside you as you discuss grief. I hope this book helps you start the conversation about grief—yours and theirs—and that it opens up a safe space to explore this topic together. This book is here to show you that grief is a natural part of being human and that we grieve as deeply as we feel and love.

Grief is a small word for a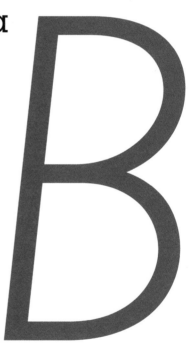

experience.

Grief

is a natural response
to loss of any kind,
and everyone feels
grief differently.

There are as many ways
to experience grief as
there are people—and
that's a lot of ways.

Sometimes,
people who are grieving
say they are in a
club.

It helps knowing you aren't alone, even though no one really wants to join this club.

You can feel grief about
a lot of things, like…

*When you lose
something meaningful.*

When a friend moves away.

When a pet dies.

When you have to change schools.

When you don't win a competition.

When a person in your life dies.

**That's the kind of grief
I want to talk about with you.**

My name is Brennan
and my mom died when
I was 12 years old.

My experience with grief started with that life-changing moment.

I'm a grownup now,
and even though it's been
many years since then,

my grief has been with me
this whole time.

Somet
feels r
hug

imes it
eally

e. Like a giant boulder
sitting on my chest.

Other times it's pretty *small.*

Like a tiny pebble in my pocket.

But it's always there with me

no matter what.

My mom, Doris,
made every day feel like
magic for me and
my family.

One time,
during a warm summer rainstorm, she put us in our swimsuits so we could go outside and play in the rain and jump in mud puddles!

She loved having fun
and always encouraged us
to live each day with

laugh

ter.

When my mom died, I was

sad,

angry,

confused,

and I felt

all alone.

I had stomachaches
and I couldn't concentrate
in school.

Some nights I couldn't sleep.
Other times, all I wanted
to do was sleep.

It seemed like the rest of the world
kept going on like nothing
had happened,

but my world had **completely stopped.**

My grief wasn't simple.
I wanted it to look like this. _____

Easy, always moving forward,
and with a clear end in sight.

But really, it was messy,
and my experience looked
more like this.

Up, down,
back and forth,
and all over the place.

And I wondered, why was this happening to me and my family?

Have you felt this way before, or maybe right now?

Or maybe

Afraid, Bad, Frustrated, Sad, Weak,
Powerless, Misunderstood, Exhausted,
Restless, Crushed, Ashamed, Somber,
Lonely, Pessimistic, Bored, Questioning,
Defeated, Selfish, Bothered, Calm,
Sick, Downhearted, Denial, Tense,
Depressed, Thoughtful, Cheated, Light,
Nauseous, Protective, Lost, Unconnected,
Overwhelmed, Unhappy, Regretful,
Compassionate, Blah, Confused, Needy,
Despair, Preoccupied, Distracted, Pain,
Embarrassed, Relieved, Disappointed,
Peaceful, Worthless, Upset, Nervous,

you feel ...

Fearful, Distressed, Sorrowful, Furious,
Giving, Tired, Reflective, Scared, Curious,
Grateful, Guilty, Heartbroken, Heavy,
Paranoid, Gloomy, Shocked, Anxiety,
Helpless, Hungry All The Time, Not
Hungry At All, Hurt, Impatient, Uneasy,
Cautious, Indecisive, Hopeful, Envious,
Indifferent, Irritated, Panicked, Livid, Joyful,
Betrayed, Love, Hostile, Mad, Worried,
Numb, Optimistic, Bitter, Proud, Quiet,
Rageful, Aggressive, Reserved, Shaky,
Miserable, Strong, Thankful, Unbelieving,
Uncertain, Motivated, Wronged, Alone...

Maybe you feel all these things.

Maybe you feel nothing at all.

Maybe you feel something
else entirely.

But whatever you feel, it's all OK.*

Because grief is natural, normal, healthy, and part of being human.

*If you feel things that are scary to you, tell a trusted grownup.

When someone we care about dies,
we miss so much about them—

the sound of their voice,

the way they smell,

the feel of their hugs,

and all the ways
they were part of our lives.

Our bodies notice
and respond to this change
by trying to adjust to the
person's absence.

That's why we can get
headaches or stomachaches,
and have trouble sleeping, eating,
relaxing, or wanting to do the same
things we're used to doing.

That's how grief works.

I learned all about grief
at a place called

Dougy Center.

It's a place where kids who are
grieving can come together to share
their experiences.*

I went there after my mom died.

*There are many places like the Dougy Center. To find one near
your community, or for more resources on children and grief,
please see the information at the end of this book.

Listening to other kids share their stories made it easier to share mine.

It helped me so much to know I wasn't the only kid in the world whose parent died.

One of the most important lessons I've learned is this:

*it's **OK** that it will never be **OK** that my mom died*.

Because acknowledging that it stinks helps me feel all of my emotions and not bottle them up.

I *still* miss my mom all the time.

I *still* cry sometimes.

I *still* have days when
I'm angry she's gone.

But I have found ways to express my grief and honor my relationship with my mom even though she's not here.

I share stories about her, think about what she would be like now, or what advice she would have given me.

I don't want to forget my mom
no matter how old I am, and
I am OK with feeling both
joy and **sadness** at once.

Now I work at a place where grieving kids come together, and I've learned a lot about what can help.

Finding ways to express your grief is a huge part of experiencing grief.

That might look like...

· dancing.

· punching a punching bag.

· watching a funny movie so you can laugh.

· calling a friend or family member.

· dribbling a ball for a really long time.

· taking a nap.

· playing a musical instrument.

· creating a scrapbook or memory box.

· going for a walk.

· trying something new.

· trying something your person loved doing.

· acting and playing dress up.

· watching a sad movie so you can cry.

· journaling, writing a letter, or writing a story...

just to name a few!

Maybe you want to try
all these things.

Maybe you're not interested
in any of these things.

Maybe you'll find something totally
different you want to do instead.

However you express your grief,* it can be really helpful to just get it out.

It can also be helpful to have someone to share your grief with—someone you can show your art to, or share your music or journal with, or who can be there when you cry.

I have also learned that,
when it comes to grief:

It is OK

to really miss the person who died and still have fun with your friends.

Laughing and playing will never mean you love them any less.

Grief is natural.

It is OK

to remember the entire person—
the good parts, the bad parts,
the funny parts, the quirky parts,
and every in-between part.

Grief is normal.

It is OK

that your grief stays with you
for the rest of your life.

You do not have to forget
or try to get over it.

Grief is healthy.

It is OK

to always remember and
love the person who died.

Grief is a part of
being human.

Grief

can be really hard.

It helps to remember that it's normal
to grieve when someone
you love is gone.

And it helps to know
we are in this club...

together.

Outro

I hope this is just the beginning of the conversations your family will have about grief. I hope this is the start of sharing a lifetime of memories, tears, and laughter when talking about the person in your kid's life who died.

Being open and honest about loss and grief with your kid will build trust—not only with you but with grownups in general. Thank you for being vulnerable and brave.

Please remember, you are not alone and neither is your kid. In fact, according to the Childhood Bereavement Estimation Model (Judi's House) 1 in 13 kids in the United States will have a parent or a sibling die before they turn 18. Even knowing how prevalent childhood bereavement is, grief is often a very isolating experience. I encourage you to not only reach out to others but to practice and model self-care. Please be gentle with yourself as you navigate this time.

For additional resources for supporting children in grief and self-care, or to find support in your area, visit Dougy Center's website at dougy.org or connect with the National Alliance for Children's Grief at childrengrieve.org.

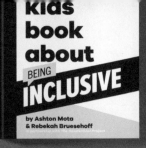
a kids book about BEING INCLUSIVE
by Ashton Mota & Rebekah Bruesehoff

a kids book about diversity
by Charnale Gordon

a kids book about LEADER SHIP
by Orion Jean

a kids book about SAFETY
by Soraya Sutherlin, CEM
in partnership with JUDY

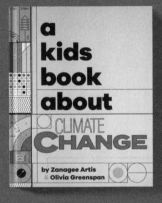
a kids book about CLIMATE CHANGE
by Zanagee Artis & Olivia Greenspan

a kids book about IMAGINATION
by LEVAR BURTON

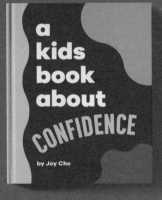
a kids book about CONFIDENCE
by Joy Cho

a kids book about ANXIETY

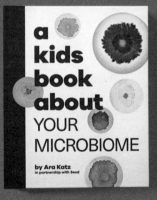
a kids book about YOUR MICROBIOME
by Ara Katz
in partnership with Seed

a kids book about racism
by Jelani Memory

a kids book about DISABILITIES
by Kristine Napper

a kids book about
by KYLE

a kids book about DIVORCE
by Ashley Simpo

a kids book about cancer
by Dr. Kelsie Storm & Sarah Porter

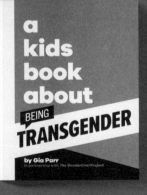
a kids book about BEING TRANSGENDER
by Gia Parr
in partnership with The GenderCool Project

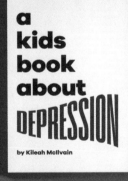
a kids book about DEPRESSION
by Kileah McIlvain

a kids book about THE TULSA RACE MASSACRE